Also by Heike Guilford:

"How to fill 50 jobs in 90 days: the recruitment blueprint for people, profit and position"

How to interview people

A guide to choosing the best person for the job every time

Heike Guilford

Note To Readers

This publication is designed to provide accurate, helpful and informative material in regard to the subject matter covered. The suggested tools and strategies covered in this book may not be suitable to everyone, and are not guaranteed or warranted to produce any particular results.

This book is sold with the understanding that the author is not engaged in rendering legal, financial, accounting, or other professional advice or services. If legal advice or other expert assistance is required, the services of a competent professional should be sought.

The author does not take any responsibility for any liability, loss or risk, personal or otherwise, which is incurred as a consequence, directly or indirectly, of the use and application of any of the contents of this book. The names of the persons appearing in this book have been changed for privacy reasons.

This publication may not be reproduced, stored in a retrieval system, or transmitted in whole or in part, in any form or by any means, electronic, mechanical, photocopying, recording, or otherwise, without prior permission of the author.

What people said after reading "How to fill 50 jobs in 90 days"

"The book is packed with some excellent tips, these include how to engage a future workforce, how to locate people, how to assess your candidate, creating an ultimate plan for action. I found this book well written and easy to follow. It is clearly researched, Heike has clearly a good grasp of the subject matter. This would be useful for any manager wanting to fill some posts. If you have posts to fill and you are having difficulty wondering how to proceed just buy the book."

-David Batemann-

"Heike is an expert in her field and her unique book will prove invaluable for healthcare providers needing to build strong teams"

-Hayley Goleniowska from Downs Side Up-

"Great book, an informative read. Useful resource for anyone wanting to recruit successfully"

-Pen Clark-

Contents

Chapter 1
How to survive on the other side of the table

There are literally thousands of books available for anyone preparing for an interview. If you are the one looking for a job that is. It's a completely different story if you are the one with the difficult task of choosing the right person for your team.

I will never forget how excited I was when I greeted my very first candidate. My one day interview training course had filled me with confidence and I was ready. Or so I thought. Nothing prepared me for the challenges I would encounter. Strangers showing up at the door with no interest of getting the job, asking me to sign their form for the benefit office. Candidates trying to negotiate a much higher salary than the one I could offer. Applicants turning up in my office filled with nerves and anxiety. I often wished I had a practical guide to figure out what to do in different circumstances.

I have lost count of the number of interviewees I met in the years to follow. I spent hours learning how to organise recruitment days, assessment centres and standard interviews for junior staff to Senior Managers. I have seen bomb disposal experts take to care work like a duck to water.

I also found resignation letters from employees having started just three days earlier.

I experienced time and time again that decisions made before, during and after an interview can make or break your team. There is also a shocking statistic from the Oxford Institute of Economics suggesting that the average cost of replacing just one person is a staggering £30,000.

I wrote this book to save you time and money. Going through the process of assessing, selecting and interviewing people gave me a chance to study what works as well as mistakes to avoid when choosing the right person for the job. I want to share with you everything I have learned so far in this practical guide.

# # #

What you will learn in this book:

This book gives you everything you need for choosing the best person for the job every single time.

You will learn all the things the standard interview training course didn't teach you. How to transform application forms into a measure of quality opposed to quantity. How to say no even if you are desperate for staff. What to do if your highly recommended candidate shows up late for interview. How to design value -based interview questions suitable to your workplace without a lengthy template to work through. What simple action you can take to create and retain a sustainable workforce for now and in the future.

How to use this book:

You can dive right in and read this book in one go, or find solutions to a particular problem you are trying to solve right now. It's completely up to you.

Take a look at the factors influencing the cycle of recruitment in Chapter 1.

In Chapter 2, explore different strategies to attract talented staff, including professionals from other industries. Discover how you can change application forms, build value -based interview questions and structure recruitment days in Chapter 3. What to do if your applicant shows up late, has a criminal record or demands more than you can give? Find the answers to all of these questions and conquer common interview challenges in Chapter 4. In Chapter 5, organise inductions and plan for the end of probationary periods. Last but not least, create a strong foundation for staff retention in Chapter 6.

Each chapter is filled with case studies, tips and short exercises to help you get the most out of this book.

I am confident that you will find new insights, ideas and sparks of inspiration right here in this book. I would like to include this short disclaimer before we start: Coaching is All About the Tools. All the strategies you find here will only be of value once you start applying them to your own situation. This may seem obvious to you. There is no need to use them all at once. Tiny tweaks in your existing systems can make a substantial difference to the effectiveness and quality of your service, in addition to your balance sheets!

Chapter 2

Recruitment essentials: Understanding KPI's

Understanding KPI's or How many people does it take to do one job?

I sat down hoping nobody would hear the sound of my heart hopping out of my chest in the conference room. Everybody was there. The CEO of the company, corporate managers, the accountant and my boss. I had been promoted to Senior Management six months earlier and this was my first operations meeting. I was heading up the largest department, or in other words, the best place to save cash and generate profits. The accountant handed out a piece of paper with numbers and pie charts on it. I felt completely out of my depth. The heading said 'Key Performance Indicators', KPI for short, with lots and lots of numbers on it. The monthly KPI sheet soon became my best friend or worst enemy, depending on the state of business. It showed a financial breakdown of new starters, leavers, sickness, training hours, annual leave, maternity leave, agency expenditure and open vacancies. There was a variance build in of 0.25%, which meant I had to recruit 1.25 people to fill one position.

Understanding this was a real game changer for me. It enabled me to plan ahead for expected absences and adjust recruitment vacancies on short notice. Looking at the numbers each month helped me identify new opportunities or areas to really focus on.

I learned that my KPIs could look shiny and pretty on Wednesday, just to take a tumble with unexpected operational demands come Thursday. You might be lucky and work in an environment of steady demands, so that you can forecast accurately your staffing needs in the upcoming months. On the other hand, you may find that your ability to meet demands fluctuates on a daily basis. Whatever the case may be, my best advice to you is just this: Get to know all the factors influencing your KPI figures.

Exercise: Understanding your KPI figures

How many people do you need to fill one vacancy?
What is your absence, sickness, training and annual leave (ASTA) variance?
What aspects of business strategy and development influence your recruitment numbers?
Examples from health -and social care: planned admissions, increase in students, emergency referrals, upcoming discharges, risk of work related injuries or new service developments.

How do you currently plan your recruitment goals? Is there anything else you need to do to manage unforeseen changes in operational needs? Are there any other people you need to consult with to maintain high standards and achieve your targets?

# # #

Recruitment circles: How to attract candidates all year round

Do you get that feeling of wanting to change your life, your body, your house...every single year in January? There seems to be something in the air at that time of year. There is also the possibility that we get hypnotised by the magazine articles telling us we deserve better, can do better and our best self is just waiting around the corner. I used to be astonished by the amount of resignation letters I would find under my door following New Year's Day. Just when I thought I had all my vacancies filled, the game would start again.

When I first became a Senior Manager, I had absolutely no idea how long it would take to employ just one person. Advertising the vacancy, going through the application forms, organising recruitment days and offering the job could all be done within four weeks. The problems started afterwards. There was the wait for criminal record checks to come through. The need to deliver comprehensive induction training followed by the chance for new starters to shadow more experienced team members. All in all, it took three months for successful candidates to turn into colleagues.

Clinical changes would impact on our staffing requirements and resignation letters would arrive all year round. I realised I had an edge over the competition once I accepted recruitment is an on-going, circular process. I worked with my team to plan activities throughout the year. We brainstormed how we could get strangers interested in our work, build a database of interested candidates and stay in touch with developments. We noticed a steep increase of direct applicants when positions became available a few months down the line.

Exercise: Planning your recruitment cycle

- What recruitment activities do you have in place all year round?
- How long is your average time frame to fill a vacancy?
- What internal and external factors influence the number of openings? Do you have planned organisational developments

or changes in clientele increasing or decreasing your operational staffing requirements?

How to build a contact base of interested and suitable candidates

I want you to cast your mind over your current recruitment strategy as it is. What is your plan to increase direct application rates and move away from agencies? If I were to hazard a guess, I would say that you are probably looking to attract staff from other industries, persuade temporary agency staff to join you, support the career development of existing staff and enhance your brand via Social Media. What option would you consider the most likely to succeed? Which one would you concentrate on to get a good return on the time and effort invested?

Personally, I believe persuading staff from other industries to jump careers is a strong contender. Think about it. The retail industry seems to be really struggling at the moment. Big brand names such as Woolworths (some years ago) or British Home Stores (more recently to this book being published) are going under. This leaves a lot of talented, skilled people without a job. Imagine they consider a career change. Somehow, they end up on your website. Reading through the information, they like what they see. Having arrived on the job page and going through the different adverts, doubt suddenly sets in. "Can I really do that job? I haven't applied for a job in 10 years, what could I possibly say on the application form? Is this career change really right for me?

Now picture this. Your colleague Mandy* used to work in a restaurant before she started her career with you. She completed her QCF qualifications and with support from the company worked her way up the ladder. She is now a team leader and absolutely loves her job. You ask her if she could write down ten tips she would give other people in the same situation she was in all those years ago. You ask your IT department to add this to your job page. People enter their e-mail address and can download Mandy's* career advice. How different would that be from the job site of your competitor? How helpful would it be to build an e-mail contact list of already interested future applicants? How much could you save, both in effort and advertising costs?

Professional marketers will tell you that creating a 'landing page' is one of the most effective ways of building an e-mail list of potential customers, clients or in this case future employees. Even if people only download the tips and don't apply, you know they are interested and you can keep them updated with any future developments. You are able to build a relationship and access a pipeline of highly desirable future applicants without spending a single penny on expensive advertising. How great is that?

One word of warning though -do not bombard people with excessive amounts of e-mail and always add the option to unsubscribe to your marketing e-mails.

Exercise: How to build a contact base of interested candidates

- What do you currently do to build a contact list of interested applicants?
- Have you got a content marketing strategy to continuously engage with future employees?
- Where are the most likely places people will get to know you and learn more about your work?
- How often do you contact previous applicants to let them know of upcoming opportunities?

- Do you have a feature on your web page allowing visitors to download a piece of helpful content in exchange for their e-mail address?

# # #

How to enhance salary —and benefit offers without breaking the bank:

Looking back over my career in healthcare stretching over twenty years, I am amazed how often I negotiated on a daily basis. Whether it's over care plans with clients, breaks with colleagues or salary requests with applicants, good bartering is now an essential part of the job description. I have seen countless applicants trip over this final hurdle. There is often noticeable discomfort on both sides of the table when it comes to talking money. It doesn't really matter how much money you can offer. What really counts is a sound strategy to make your offerings go all the way to the signed contract.

Let's take a look at some common scenarios:

Josephine is a manager looking to recruit two new team members. She can offer a salary between £25,000-£32,000 per annum, depending on experience. The average pay for her existing staff is £27,800.
Daniel has six months experience in the field. Josephine offers him the baseline salary of £25,000. Daniel accepts and they shake hands at interview.

It's two weeks later and Mark is attending his interview. He comes highly recommended and has three years' experience. His statutory and mandatory training is all up to date. He shows Josephine additional training he has completed to develop specialist skills relevant to the open position. He does not shy away from discussing his wage expectations. Mark is asking for £32,000. Josephine offers £29,000 and Mark counters with £31,000. He tells her that there are other offers on the table for him. He informs Josephine that he is ready to walk away and straight up to the door of the competition, if she doesn't pay what he is asking for.

Josephine feels torn. She likes what Mark brings to the table. She also knows that wages get discussed among team members and worries about the potential fallout. Josephine seeks advice from her colleague in the HR department, who suggests that Mark might be interested in additional training.

In the end, Josephine agrees with Mark to pay for one additional course and £30,000 salary. Josephine knows that the knowledge Mark brings back from the training course will be a real asset to her team and the organisation as a whole. Mark accepts the new offer. Josephine and Mark have managed to reach a mutual agreement, leaving both parties satisfied with the outcome.

Exercise:

Consider both scenarios. What do you believe is a fair salary for each candidate? Can you think of other bargaining chips to use in interview negotiations?

What value you are able to offer apart from salary alone? Knowledge is power and the majority of candidates want to develop their skills. You might be able to leverage your healthy training budget to sway desirable applicants. You could also integrate the development of specialist skills for newcomers and existing staff as part of your brand building strategy. This is of particular benefit if you want to present at events or conferences.

Analyse how your investment in training could pay off in different ways. For example, you might secure a motivated candidate by offering to fund mentorship training. This in turn could open doors with local universities sending students for placements. It could also help you implement a buddy -mentorship program between junior and more experienced staff. All of these activities will support the growth of a sustainable workforce within your organisation.

Examples of other bargaining chips:

Flexible working agreements or shifts
Ability to leave the workplace in break time
Complimentary tea and coffee
Canteen or local amenities within walking distance
Flexible office hours
Ability to work from home
Development of specialist skills -and knowledge base combined with a shared learning plan.

Think about your workplace. What tangible and intangible benefits can you offer?
What impact will the introduction of the minimum wage have on your ability to negotiate?

Chapter 3

How to find great people in the first place

How to recruit staff from other industries

"When I learned that my job was going to be made redundant, I felt angry, shocked and sad. It didn't help that I was still recovering from having extensive treatment to remove a benign tumour. I had no idea what to do next and my confidence had hit rock bottom. I had been working in healthcare for over 15 years. Being a nurse, climbing the career ladder, advancing into management...I couldn't understand how all of my dreams had turned into this nightmare. After moping around for a couple of weeks, I started to really miss going to work. I knew I didn't want to go back into Senior Management. I researched different career options and decided to start all over again. I had no idea that obtaining coaching -and teaching qualifications, setting up my own coaching practice in addition to specialising my work would allow me to realise my childhood dream of becoming a writer. I discovered that it's possible for me to still work as a nurse whilst teaching, coaching, training and writing. I am grateful that I can look back and see that my redundancy opened up a whole range of options I hadn't thought about before."

Going through redundancy allowed me to put myself in the shoes of job seekers working in other fields. Although it is different for everyone, there are common traits shared during this experience. I discovered that anger, sadness, fear, frustration and the longing for change are all emotions we go through during this life changing event. Being able to relate to this experience will give you a great starting point when planning your own pitch to attract staff from other industries.

Exercise: How to plan your pitch and attract staff with transferable skills

Take a step back and pretend you are working for a major cooperation in the service industry. Work is fun and you are earning a great wage. You have just re-mortgaged your house to give the kitchen a much needed make -over. Your kids are loving pre-school and your wife has just found a part -time job to earn a little extra cash. Arriving for your shift on Monday morning, you are informed by a Senior Manager that the company is now automating the majority of tasks, resulting in 50% of the workforce being laid off.

- How would you feel in this situation?
- What would you do after the initial anger has worn off?
- Where would you go looking for work?
- What skills, knowledge, experience and expertise do you have that could be transferred to another environment?
- When was the last time you applied for a job? Would you be familiar with completing your application form online?
- What do you need to know before you can decide whether or not you want to completely leave your industry?
- How far would you be willing to travel?

Writing down the answers to all of these questions will give you the perspective you need to build a powerful pitch.

# # #

How to save your advertising budget with candidate profiles

Who do you really want working for you? The job description and person specification combined are a bit like a wish list, spelling out your ideal candidate. It tells you the qualities, characteristics, skills, qualifications and knowledge required of someone to not only do the job, but do it well. While all of this information is helpful, it doesn't give you any idea of where to find this person in the first place.

Studying this a little more can really elevate your recruitment campaigns and enhance your chance of success further down the line. If you need someone with experience in the field, where would you find them right now? What knowledge and skills are they looking to develop further? What would persuade them to join <u>your</u> team?

Exercise: Profiling your ideal candidate

- Imagine you are working in the job you are hoping to fill. Who would you be working for if you are living in the local area?
- Do you work in the private, public or charity sector?
- Would this job be a step up in your career? If it is on the same level, why would you be interested in this position?
- Is your vacancy an entry level position, for example care assistant job? How could taking this job change your career prospects in the future? Are there opportunities to further your career to a degree level through work-based apprenticeships for example?
- Do you have transferrable skills you could bring to the job? Have you been recently made redundant, maybe from the retail sector, and you are searching for your next challenge?

- What are your personal circumstances? Are you a single mum? Is it important to you to have flexibility over your working hours or do you like working in a set pattern, like a rota?

You may have noticed during this process that the question of salary did not feature on the list, and wonder why. The reason is simple. Studies have shown that money is not the deciding factor when it comes to choosing a new position. In fact, in the studies, the need for personal happiness and fulfilment came in first, followed by the desire to make a difference. When I share these findings with my course participants, reactions often vary. While some nod in agreement, others immediately tell me that they would definitely follow the money.

Asked if they would leave their current position for a new opportunity offering £10,000 more in annual salary, students often hesitate. "What's the catch?" is often the next question they ask, followed by an analysis of potential pitfalls, risks and benefits.

When people show up for interview, they will be going through the same process. When you anticipate the needs of your applicants, you can show them how you can help them reach their goals. Doing this will allow you to enhance the effectiveness of your communications at every step of the way. Your candidate will positively engage with you and your offerings, from advert to interview.

# # #

How to make sure your desirable candidate picks you

Today is a busy day for you. Checking e-mails between meetings, returning phone calls, making time for staff knocking on your door asking for advice. Somehow time is running much quicker than usual and before you know it, your receptionist calls to tell you your interviewee has arrived. On the way out of your door, a colleague is asking 'Can I just have a moment of your time?"

Read any book on preparing for interviews and you learn that you must never, ever be late for a future employee. If you think back when you went for the interview for your current job, how early did you show up? Getting to an interview on time is just as important when the shoe is on the other foot. Giving your candidate a positive experience of you and your company has a multitude of benefits. You make a good impression, build brand awareness and get people talking for all the right reasons.

We all have busy days, and we all know that feeling when there just isn't enough time in the day for everything. A candidate coming for a job interview may have turned into a rather routine task in your schedule. You already know what is going to happen. The room is prepared, your colleague is ready, there is a quick tour around the place, a presentation, you ask your questions, you give your candidate the chance to get the information they need, discuss salary...job done.

No problem, right? Wrong!
It's important to remember that skilled, experienced and talented staff are usually in short supply, no matter what industry you are working in. This means that whoever comes knocking on your door will have lined up more than one appointment. If that person is a good fit, you want to leave a great impression, so that they sign a contract with you. Giving into the temptation of going through the motions can lead to costly mistakes, as your concentration slips and your mind wanders off.

Exercise: How to make a great impression

- Write down all the things you currently do when interviewing candidates. Do you organise recruitment days or do you schedule individual interviews?
- How much time does it take to conduct a single interview? Don't forget the time you will need to set up a room, arrange for colleagues to sit in, review your interview questions, meet and greet your candidate, etc.
- Once you know how much time you need, make sure you schedule it in your diary!
- Is your place easy to find with a navigation system or map? We have all been there - you type an address into your satnav, you follow all the directions to the letter and you end up some place completely different. I used to work in a place, where the postcode just typed into the satnav would take you to the nearest cemetery instead of our company! Obviously, you don't want that to happen to anyone! If your workplace is off the beaten track or tricky to locate, consider sending out directions with the invitation letter.
- Do you give your candidate a tour around? What do you really want them to see, hear and feel? Who do you want them to meet? Don't forget, the people you really want need to be convinced that you are a good fit for them!
- Ask three trusted colleagues about their past interview experiences. What do they remember? What were key factors when they made their decision of signing on the dotted line?

What else could you do to ensure you are able to meet and greet your candidates at the scheduled time-every time?

#

How to engage your staff in recruitment

"I really didn't know if this job was going to be for me. I only ever worked in pubs and clubs before I applied for this. I got a lot of training and really connected with the clients. I really look forward to work each day, as every day is very different. I decided to take part in additional training courses offered to me by the company. I got promoted to team leader a year ago. I'm loving it so much, I'm looking to progress my career even further here. I would never go back to my old job"

Anna* had the audience completely mesmerised. Her story particularly resonated with candidates hoping to change their career into something more fulfilling. There were also a number of people, who just got made redundant from the service industry. They too had paid careful attention and asked a number of questions at the end.

Most candidates come to their interview day excited about the prospect of a fresh start, new challenges and opportunities. But they are also full of doubt. They are looking for reassurance that your place is a good place for them. Applicants will want to know that they will be happy working for you. You can do this by providing assurance from people they can relate to and trust.

This is particularly true if you want to attract and recruit staff from other industry sectors. Many of them will have transferrable skills and knowledge they can bring to the job. What they won't have though is confidence that they can succeed in a field they know nothing about.

Exercise: How to build confidence and trust in your company and your team

Do you have staff with a similar background to your candidate(s) working for you? Would they be willing to give a short presentation, maybe as part of recruitment days or assessment centres, to your candidates? Could you ask them to take part in a short video, talking about their journey, that you could use for your website and other marketing material?

Hot tip: Look at some of your competitors' websites. Do they already have these kind of videos on their site? Watch the video and ask yourself: Does it look authentic? Do you believe what this person is telling you? If you have no idea about the sector, the job or the challenges ahead, would you be persuaded enough to pick up the application form?

Chapter 4
Strategies for assessment & selection

The last barrier to selection

What started out with a plain letter inviting you to an interview for your dream job has somehow become the stuff of nightmares. The stack of problems you are about to face seems as high as the mountain that you and 199 other candidates are peering up, in the hope of landing the job.

The pouring rain drenches your clothes, together with your backpack. What was once a small footpath right on the edge of the cliff has morphed into one long mudslide. The sound of raindrops fails to silence the unruly voice in your head torn between the desire to reach your goal and the temptation to stop right here, right now. You have worked hard to come this far. Superhuman effort propels you one step forward. Relief, coupled with fear, washes over you when you see the finish line. Crossing it will mean either total failure or complete victory. No need to wait for a phone call or a letter to see if you've made the grade. You will know if you are going home empty handed or join the elite SAS force in just a few more seconds...

"Many try to get into the Special Air Service (SAS) regiment. Most of them fail. Out of an average intake of 125 candidates, the gruelling selection process will weed out all but 10." (Taken from www.eliteforces.info/speical-air-service/sas-selection/)

I told this story in my first book "How to fill 50 jobs in 90 days" to demonstrate how different organisations assess and select applicants. Of course, your ability to rigorously test and asses your future employees is pretty much a matter of supply and demand. You are more likely to introduce though selection methods if you have talented people queueing outside your door. You may be more apprehensive if you don't have enough applications to choose from as it is.

The SAS have a thorough selection process for a reason. Recruitment for them is literally a matter of life and death. What are the consequences of giving the job to the wrong person for you? Perhaps it's just money if it's a one-off event. Let it happen just a few more times over the course of a year, and you could be facing serious organisational and financial constraints.

Regardless of your current situation, I would encourage you to carefully plan out the last barrier to success within your recruitment process.

# # #

What to look out for when reviewing CV's and application forms

I remember how excited I was when I first started to review CV's and application forms. It was interesting to see whether applicants had read the full instructions, completed all the sections and used black ink. It was the time before online forms and deciphering some peoples handwriting felt a bit like breaking a code. Some forms would provide me with more questions than answers. People with a pattern of changing jobs every six months, the box for disciplinary action ticked or a criminal history would set alarm bells ringing.

It's understandable that job seekers do not want to tell you the full story. Fearing they won't get selected for an interview, they often miss out key pieces of information.

This can make assessing applicants particularly difficult. Even someone with great skills and knowledge will have a hard time getting to the next stage if they hop from job to job. Candidates with criminal convictions could present a real risk to your organisation. Weighing up these risks is vital at this point of the process and could save you significant cash later down the line. I was not exactly thrilled when my HR colleague proposed we use a formal assessment form with a point system to analyse and evaluate future colleagues in a more objective manner. However, I soon changed my mind. Using this new method made decisions a whole lot easier. I went through the form and carefully scored points for things like:

Are all sections completed correctly including personal details?
Do we have an application form or CV only?
If handwritten, is the handwriting legible and black ink used?
Has the candidate previous experience and skills transferrable to this position?
Has the candidate completed additional training courses relating to the job description?
If criminal cautions and convictions is ticked, do we have further details?

I observed a real change in the quality of applicants showing up for recruitment process after just one month of using the form. Although it was difficult to say no to a higher number of people, it proved of real benefit in the long run.

Exercise: Assessing your application forms

- Before you start assessing application forms, ask yourself: How much time do you realistically need to clear out of your diary for this? Is it something you need to do every day, once a week or on an ad-hoc basis?

- Do you have any formalised tools or scoring matrix you can use to aid your decision-making process?

- Have you got a parameter for saying yes or no to candidates involved in disciplinary procedures and/or criminal convictions? This is important as you may find yourself in quite a few moral dilemmas. If someone committed a burglary 20 years ago with no incidents since, would you give them a chance? Would you select a person with points on their license for speeding over the person driving under the influence? Your decision- making process may be very clear cut. If it isn't, you may want to liaise with your colleagues and line manager to set up a more systematic approach for this.

# # #

How to design scenario-and value based interview questions

If the plant in your house could talk, what would it say about your organisational skills? When was the last time you asked that interview question?

There are now countless books helping your potential future colleagues prepare for interview. They give candidates the most commonly asked questions, frameworks and suggest ways to answer the questions. This reality combined with you asking the same set of questions again and again can easily lead to complete interview fatigue. The world of HR has certainly recognised this and there are now a multitude of tools out there to help you design your questions. Most of them recommend the use of value-based interview questions as they are less predictable. Frameworks are certainly a great way to introduce structure into your line of questioning. Personally, I prefer real life scenario questions. They offer the opportunity to assess thoroughly the reasoning of your candidate. At the same time, they are invaluable to give you more insights into someone's character and personality.

Alice* came for a qualified nurse interview. We were nearing the end of our questions. Everything had gone swimmingly so far and I was already feeling elated. We finally had found a fabulous nurse with plenty of knowledge, experience, skills and get up and go. Only two more questions to go…

"Imagine you are attending a review meeting for one of your clients. When you enter the room, one of the external professionals has collapsed in his chair and appears to be unresponsive. What would you do?"
Alice thought for a moment before responding.
'I am a qualified mental health nurse. This is clearly a medical issue and therefore not my problem. I would try to call one of the doctors and tell them to deal with it!"

"You wouldn't start CPR after calling for assistance?"

"No, like I said -I'm not a medical professional. This is outside my field of expertise!"

Alice sounded incredibly confident in her answers. My colleague and I exchanged looks. We had just spent the last month training our nursing team in CPR skills and even set up weekly practice sessions. None of our nurses were generally trained. Our client group had very complex health needs and we wanted nurses to be able to support them.

We finished up the interview and discussed our options. On one hand, Alice brought a wealth of knowledge, having worked in a variety of settings. Her theoretical knowledge of legislation and regulation was second to none. But that CPR question was really bugging us. What would happen if she really stumbled upon a real -life crisis? Would she just wash her hands of it, saying that the issue was outside of her remit of expertise?
We decided to say no and keep looking.

As you can see, there is a reason why scenario questions do not have a right or a wrong answer as such. How you feel about someone's response is influenced by a number of factors. Your own moral fibre, your personal values and beliefs as well as current organisational challenges all impact your decision-making processes.

Exercise: Building value based interview questions

- Start by asking six members of your team about the most common challenges presented in a normal workday. What strategies do your colleagues use to overcome these? Could you turn them into a scenario question to use at interview?

- What do you really want to know about someone? It's easy for people to talk about their strengths and weaknesses as this is really one of the most universal questions asked. It's more difficult for candidates to think through a situation, analyse their options and tell you how they would solve this particular problem.

- Remember to review your scenario questions regularly. Staff tend to recommend good workplaces to their friends. It's likely that they will share what they know and can remember about the recruitment process. Introducing 3-4 new questions every 12 weeks will keep your spirits up and eliminate the risk of cloned answers.

How to ditch boring questions and find out what you really want to know

How would your former boss describe your ability to handle stressful situations ? When was the last time you asked that question?
With thousands of interview books predicting the most commonly asked questions, it's hard to come up with something different. Of course, asking the same old thing over and over again is not only boring, it will also not give you the answers you really want.
Why not try giving your standard interview template a little makeover?

Let's play: Ask this, not that

Ask this: What would people closest to you describe as your best characteristic?
Not that: What are your strengths and weaknesses?

Ask this: What aspects of the job do you think you will enjoy the most?
Not: Why do you want this position?

Ask this: Can you give me an example of a recent problem you've had. What steps did you take to solve it?
Not: How do you deal with challenging situations?

Ask this: If the plant in your house could talk, what would she tell me about your ability to cope with stress?
Not: How do you cope with stress?

Ask this: How would you notice that it's time to ask for help when things are not going to plan?
Not: How do you cope with failure?

Exercise:

Take a look at all of your standard, predictable interview questions. How could you change them around based on these examples?

# # #

How to organise brilliant interview –and recruitment days

Organising whole recruitment days or assessment centres can seem a bit excessive when you have a lot of work on and you are pressured to hit your financial targets. You could also save a small fortune if are able to link all of your recruitment activities to your staff retention goals.

Recruitment days turned into a real asset for me when I observed that candidates jumped at the chance of learning more about their future colleagues, and existing staff wanted to get to know potential team members early on. The greatest benefit of was a significant increase in staff staying with us for 12 months and beyond.

Exercise: How to plan recruitment days

- Decide on the basic components of the day. This may be registration and coffee followed by a presentation, practical exercises such as case studies with team discussion, a tour round facilitated by colleagues, the interview and finally evaluation of the day.

- Consider what skills, knowledge, characteristics and competencies you are looking for when devising case studies, observations or practical exercises. What can you set up and how can you measure success or failure objectively? Could you set up a scoring system?

- Risk assess <u>everything</u>! It doesn't matter what industry you are working in, your risk assessment for the day has to be done!

- Find willing helpers from your team and if possible different departments. A loyal member of staff sharing all the reasons they enjoy working for you can greatly influence your candidate's choices. Offering a short overview of a typical day will allow applicants to picture themselves already loving the job.

- Decide on the key goal of your presentations. Every speech is designed to move people towards taking action. Be clear what you want candidates to feel and do once they've listened to your talk.

- Download your free checklist and cheat sheet to help you plan brilliant interviews and recruitment days right here: www.goagencyfree.com/recruitment-day

# # #

Why you should ask for a presentation

Dani* walked to the front of the room and showed us a picture of monkeys. It was the most unusual beginning to a presentation on leadership I've ever seen. Curious to where this was going, my colleague and I followed Dani's* pictures and explanations with great interest. When Dani* finished her talk, we had learned that she was a confident public speaker, had creativity and could engage strangers very quickly. We got all of these insights before asking a single question.

The decision to add a 10-15 minute talk to the recruitment process for junior managers and above was not an easy one. How can you put an extra hurdle in place when you are desperate for staff? Would candidates simply choose to go with a competitor?

There was a time when only Senior Managers had to stand up in front of a crowd. Those days are over. Staff on any level can be put on the spot by corporate managers, inspectors or clients. You don't want to find out at an important meeting that your colleague is brilliant at writing reports, but terrified of public speaking.

Do's and don't's when asking for a presentation:

- Do offer a choice of topics. When deciding on your topics, think about assessing your candidates' competencies and knowledge base. Have there been recent changes in legislation? Are you looking for a new way to solve recurring leadership challenges?
- Do give sufficient advance notice when sending out the interview invitation. This seems very obvious. However, if you are using agencies to source candidates, they may push you for appointments on short notice.

- Do provide any equipment that may be needed and ask candidates what they will need on the day. You may already have a room with a projector, whiteboard and flip chart already set up.
- Do remember to smile encouragingly. You may see on TV stern faces when people have to pitch or give a talk. Obviously, this will induce panic and fear. You, on the other hand, want to make this a pleasant experience and ease their nerves right away.

Don't:

- Don't forget to ask any follow-up questions after the presentation
- Don't drift off if a presentation doesn't rock your boat. While this may be the hundredth time you've heard about leadership, remember it is the first time for your candidate.
- Don't interrupt your candidate in the middle of their talk. Make a note and ask later.
- Don't set up the equipment at the last minute. Apart from looking very disorganised and unprofessional, it is very unnerving for everyone present.

# # #

Informal assessments: When coffee meets interview

"We would like you to meet for an informal chat over coffee."
I was somewhat surprised when I got this response back after applying for a director's position. Unsure what to make of it, I typed 'Coffee interview' into Google. I learned that many employers choose to set up these meetings as a way of getting to know more about a person without the stuffiness of a conference room. They may also be used when there is no clear job description in place, and HR Managers are putting out their feelers for new talent.

Here are some do's and don't's if you want to add coffee interviews to your recruitment strategy:

Do:

- Do organise the meeting at a venue outside your current workplace. A coffee shop is obviously the most logical place. If you can, avoid busy pubs, restaurants or clubs as a first meeting place. Your whole conversation could be drowned out by the noise around you.
- Do develop the questions you want to ask. There will be a need to review your current questions and adapt them to a more relaxed setting. You could always ask candidates about their hobbies on the application form and talk about their interests to calm nerves and break the ice.
- Do decide on your goals for this meeting. What are you hoping to accomplish in this meeting? What specific outcomes do you want to achieve? How will you know if your coffee date is a success?
- Do be ready and prepared for any questions your candidate has for you. Remember to create free-flowing dialogue rather than a carefully crafted interrogation.
- Do think about how you can make a good impression. Experienced and skilled candidates will always be in high demand, regardless of your industry. How can you highlight all the positive factors about your organisation and present your workplace in the best possible light?
- Do consider telling the story of you and your career. Stories have been used for centuries as a means of connecting over common ground. Cast your mind back of your first day. What motivated you to try out for your position? How is your workplace different from all the other organisations out there?

- Do have fun. This is not the time to be all stern and serious. Being able to share a little about you and your personality is one of the key advantages of being away from the office. This will give your future employee the chance to see if and how they fit into the culture.

Don't:

- Don't be tempted to fall back into full interviewing mode. Remember that this is the first step in your recruitment process. No one is expecting you to make a decision there and then.
- Don't just talk about work related topics. Let your personality shine through and get an idea of how your candidate's personality would fit into your team.
- Don't order alcohol if you can help it. The majority of workplaces do not allow the consumption of alcohol within working hours. Some employers use the restaurant or pub as a test to see if their applicant orders a beer, sticks with lemonade or follows suit by asking for whatever you are having. Consider this though. Would you really think of your workplace or future boss as very professional if they asses your suitability for the job over a beer? I appreciate that there may well be industries, where this is the norm and completely acceptable. Ultimately the choice is yours.
- Don't forget to pick up the tab. This should go without saying!
- Don't leave your candidate in the dark. Let them know the next steps. When can they expect to hear back from you? What would be the next step?

Chapter 5
Common interview challenges

Should you interview the late candidates?

Questionnaires copied, room prepared, colleague happy to help me between 2.00pm -3.00pm -everything and everyone was ready for my interview with Sophie. Or so I thought. 2pm came and went. Calling reception 15 minutes later, I really hoped that Sophie* had arrived for her nurse interview. No such luck. Maggie, our receptionist assured me that she would call me immediately when she turned up. 2.30pm came around and still no phone call, no arrival and no signs that Sophie would ever arrive. I left a message on her answerphone and informed my colleague that the interviewee appeared to be a no-show. I was engrossed in paperwork and had all but forgotten about the interview, when Maggie announced that Sophie had turned up- 2 hours late. My thoughts were racing. We were desperate for nurses, no doubt about that. On the other hand, did we really need someone, who wouldn't even pick up the phone to let us know they were having trouble getting there in time? I also was due to finish work 30 minutes later.

Sophie was full of explanations and apologies. The child minder had let her down. The car had a flat tire on the motorway. Her phone battery was flat. The more she kept talking, the more suspicious I got. How many misfortunes could one person really have in one day? I explained that we could not facilitate her interview that day and offered her another appointment a week later. Unsurprisingly, she did not turn up for that one at all.

I've learned that although every interviewee knows they should show up on time to make a good impression, not all of them do. Some may call to inform you of a dire emergency preventing them from coming. Others will cite childcare needs, broken down tires or simply getting lost as plausible explanations for standing you up. So what do you do if you have plenty of open vacancies, but don't want to compromise too much?

Do agree with your line manager a time frame for interviews, plus a buffer zone. Mine used to be 30 minutes, but it really depends on your individual preferences.

Do call your candidate if they are late to check if they are on their way.

Do not let your emotions get the better of you. You may be really annoyed with someone for wasting your time. Always be professional and stick with your agreed boundaries.

Don't feel like you have to interview late candidates just because your vacancies need to be filled. If someone is an hour late, you do need to ask yourself how important the job really is to them.

Don't take it personally. I had many candidates not turning up without any explanation whatsoever. This can feel quite disheartening, especially when you have put a lot of effort in. Keep up your spirits. It's possible the job was not right for them or they were not a good fit for you. It may sound harsh, but there is really no need to give up any of your precious time to dwell on it.

# # #

When your candidate is a bundle of nerves

I was looking forward to Katy* turning up for her interview. With a glowing CV, plenty of industry expertise and years of working in challenging healthcare settings, Katy seemed like the perfect fit for our team. There was just the small matter of the interview, but I did not anticipate any problems. Unfortunately, life always happens when you are busy making other plans and this was no exception. Katy* rushed into reception like a whirlwind. Tripping over her words, she hurriedly explained that she missed the bus and was worried that she would be late. I took her to the meeting room and offered her a drink, thinking that this would ease her nerves. Katy* gulped down a glass of water, before hurriedly starting her presentation. We couldn't persuade her to catch a breath, and the whole situation turned into a hot mess.

There is no denying that every interview meeting is a test situation. It conjures images of formality, serious faces and the need to be on best behaviour, no matter what. Naturally, this produces a great deal of anxiety combined with the fear of failing. All of this can lead to talented candidates showing up disguised as a bundle of nerves. Of course, there are organisations that put candidates under pressure to test their resilience and resolve on purpose. It's really up to you.

Here are some tried-and tested stress busting strategies:

- Include a question about candidate's interests and hobbies on the application form. Engage your candidate in small talk when you first meet them by talking about one of their preferred topics.
- Smile when you introduce yourself and offer a hot or cold beverage.

- Show candidates the bathroom and give them the opportunity to use it before the start of the meeting.
- Arrange for colleagues helping you with the interview to be in the room already to avoid unnecessary delays.
- Start the interview by asking a simple question, for example: 'We would like to start with your presentation. What is your chosen topic?"
- Take candidates on a tour around the place before the interview. Just the simple act of walking will have a calming effect.
- Have a water jug and glasses at the ready and encourage applicants to help themselves during the meeting.
- Don't interrupt candidates if they are thinking for a long time after you've asked a question. Offer to re-phrase the question if candidates are struggling to respond.

# # #

How to deal with runaway interview answers

"I just want to help people"
Oh no. I nearly groaned out loud. Why, oh why was everyone giving me the same answer when I asked "Why do you want to work here?"
If you are interviewing applicants on a regular basis, you probably have your own personalised range of runaway answers. Short of altering all the questions, what do you do when you just can't cope with hearing the same old platitudes over and over again?

How to break the pattern:

"I just want to help people" or "I just want to make a difference" are non -specific statements. If you think about it, your definition of helping someone could be poles apart. Every action has an equal reaction. This would suggest that everything you do, good or bad, will have an impact on something or someone. Asking follow up questions will allow you to learn more about their true motivation.

Example: *"I just want to make a difference"*

Possible follow up questions:

What kind of change do you want to create?
How can you be sure you have made a difference in someone's life?
What is your own personal understanding of leading positive change and can you give an example?

Exercise:

Take a look at your current interview questions and most common responses. Make a list of statements triggering a desire to roll your eyes, groan out loud or runaway.
How could you rephrase the question and generate new insights? What is the purpose of your question in the first place? How can you change the words and discover more about their personality, values, beliefs or attitude?

# # #

Awful candidates: Can you skip a question or two?

"Why do you want to work for us?" Marian looked up to the ceiling for inspiration before replying "The job centre sent me here. Could you just sign this piece of paper, so I get my benefits?"
My colleague and I exchanged baffled looks. What to do? There was no doubt that Marian had no interest at all in securing the job. Was

there any point in continuing with the interview?

I excused myself and consulted my colleague from Human Resources. She advised me that it is acceptable to explain that this was clearly not a good fit and send her on her way.

Terminating interviews is never a desirable thing to do and should be a rare occasion rather than the norm. It is possible to stop the interview once it transpires that your candidate can't meet your expectations. This saves time for both parties. Leaving early also works both ways. I used to hire staff for challenging positions. I was very aware that this was not everybody's cup of tea. I gave examples of difficult situations our workforce encounter on a daily basis. I explained that being here was a bit like Marmite-you either love it or you hate it! I reiterated to candidates that it was perfectly fine to leave if they thought this was not a good match for them. I also said that we may do the same the other way around if they were not a good fit for us. This always set us up well for the day and there were no hard feelings when we had to part ways sooner than expected.

# # #

The great candidate with the terrible DBS record

"Have you got any criminal cautions or convictions?"

"Yes!"

It never failed to amaze me how many people came to interview, admitting that they had entries in their DBS record. Pretty much all of them had they answered "No" on the application form.

This often left us with moral dilemmas. There was the person, who had a conviction for breaking and entering from 20 years ago. The talented nurse in trouble for benefit fraud. The junior manager caught with drugs in his possession. All of them would tell us that they wanted to get at least selected for interview. None of them thought this was possible if they were truthful from the very beginning. Is it fair to not give them a chance at all?

There is not really a black and white answer to this. Your company is likely to have their own code of practice with advice and guidance for handling this situation. It's vital to know them inside and out, as you may need to justify your decisions to internal - and external - stakeholders in the future.

# # #

What the friendly recruitment consultant doesn't want you to know

If your applicant has been referred by a recruitment consultancy, be wary of what's to come. Obviously, not all agents are the same and there are good eggs among them for sure. Unfortunately, most of them work on commission, so don't be surprised if you encounter any of the following scenarios:

Joe* interviewed very well for the team leader position. He had a wealth of relevant experience, great people skills and we really wanted him to work for us. When I enquired about his wage expectations, I was relieved to hear that they were well within our means. I spoke to the recruitment consultant and explained the benefit package we would like to offer. The agent on the other end of the phone went through a spiel of how much Joe liked our place and how interested he was in the position. I could feel a "but' coming on..."But Joe had other interviews lined up, already got other offers on the table, so the only way to get him would be to pay £3,000 more in annual salary.

I gave this some thought and talked it over with my colleagues. If we would go this high, he would be the top earner compared to all the other team leaders already employed. Even though he was great on paper and brilliant at interview, it was still a big risk.

I explained to the agent that Joe had been happy with the offerings on the table and we would not change our offer. Joe signed on the dotted line a short while later. When he started work, I did ask him about the wage negotiations. I was surprised to learn that Joe had not pushed for any more money and there had been no other offers on the table at all. I learned from my colleague in the HR department that recruitment agents generally get a percentage of the agreed annual salary as their commission. This means that the more you pay, the more they earn!

Annie* was a brilliant nurse. She quickly became an integral part of the crew, even though she had only been with us for three short months. Everything was going well for her, or so I thought. I had virtually just signed off her probation paperwork when her resignation letter landed on my desk. She wanted to leave to pursue new opportunities. Alarm bells started to ring. The exact same thing had already happened twice this year. I discovered that recruitment agencies charge their fee on signing of the contract. However, there is a caveat. Employers can claim back a percentage if the signed candidate leaves in the first three months. Some agents will tempt their previous clients with shiny new vacancies in the hope that the same person will earn them a commission cheque over and over again!

# # #

Money talks: What you want to think about

"What are your expectations in terms of salary?"
Tom*, who had interviewed brilliantly, replied with confidence "£30,000".

HIs number was right on the top of our salary range. I countered with £27,500 and additional training courses. He declined and explained that he had other interviews lined up and was sure someone would meet his expectations. Accepting his demands would mean that he would earn more than loyal managers, who had been with us a number of years. Yes, his CV was exemplary. Yes, he had passed all of the assessment with flying colours. And yes, losing the chance of getting him on board was painful. But what if he didn't live up to expectations? What if his colleagues discovered how much he earned and stormed into my office demanding the same deal, threatening to abscond to the competition if I didn't meet their demands?

I summarised everything that was on the table for Tom*. The salary of £27,500 linked to a competency framework. Personal - and professional - development opportunities, a sound preceptorship framework as well as the chance to become an expert in a chosen topic and present at local conferences. After accepting our offer, Tom* gradually earned the respect and trust of his peers. Progressing up the career ladder, he surpassed his original salary demand and became one of our most loyal employees.

Money talks seem to fall in either one of these three categories: candidates reluctant to even broach the topic, confident applicants seeking top dollar and future employees willing to negotiate a favourable deal for both parties. Everybody loves a bargain and business negotiations, although daunting, are no different. You want to walk away, knowing you got great value for the best price.

Exercise: How to negotiate with candidates

- What does someone really want? New parents struggling to balance work with caring for their baby may place more value on flexible working arrangements than hourly pay. Anyone coming to you previously affected by work related stress would be likely to welcome the yoga classes included in the subsidised gym membership. Aspiring career flyers will be keen to climb the ladder and build on their existing skills and knowledge. Having a sense of personal fulfilment could be a deal maker or breaker for people coming to you from other industry sectors.

- Take stock of all of your assets: Salary, annual leave entitlement, flexible working hours or regular shift patterns, additional training, mentorship, preceptorship, gaining specialist expertise, subsidised meal provisions, loyalty bonus payments, competency based frameworks linked to earnings, career clinics for new and existing staff, free support systems are all tradable commodities.

- Know how far you will go: Have you ever paid premium price for something that completely failed to meet your expectations? It's easy to get carried away if you desperately need someone and talented staff show up at your door. There is also the fall out to consider if you agree to pay a new starter more than employees on the same level. Set yourself boundaries and stick to them. You may suffer some disappointments, but your long-term gains will far outweigh any short -term losses.

- Achieve a win-win situation: No one likes the feeling that they got ripped off. Everyone wants to walk away feeling like a winner. We all want to change our lives for the better. Focusing on how you can help applicants achieve their personal dreams and professional aspirations will go a long way towards getting talented people on board.

# # #

How to support internal candidates

My eyes widened and my heart skipped a beat when I saw the latest jobs advertised on the internal notice board. There it was: the Head of Department position had become available. I was working as a team leader at the time. Would I really have the courage to skip a step and reach the top of the career ladder? There was only one way to find out. I arranged an appointment with my boss to ask her if I even had a chance. Caroline* explained that there was a lot to learn for this new position. Understanding regulatory requirements, dealing with contract commitments, more involvement in quality control...I frantically wrote down absolutely everything she told me that morning. She finished up by saying that yes, she thought I had potential.

I ventured out of her office and completed my application form the very same day. I studied, practiced and passed the personality test. I delivered my presentation, managed to get through the interview and scenario role play before a final IQ test. I got home feeling satisfied with my performance. I was over the moon when I got offered the role the very next day.

My career has gone from strength to strength since then, but I never forgot what Caroline* did for me. Her solid advice and encouragement allowed me to succeed against the odds.
In the years to follow, I had plenty of opportunity to give back and offer the same encouragement to junior managers arriving in my office. Some colleagues soaked up everything I told them like a sponge. They were gracious, even if they didn't get the position in the end. Other colleagues were convinced that meeting with them meant the job was theirs and the assessment centre just a necessary formality. Of course, there was always disappointment when 8 people applied, 4 got short listed and only one person got promoted. This inevitably led to threats of formal complaints or resignations.

All of these experiences taught me that good intentions are not enough. Supporting internal candidates requires a delicate balance of giving encouragement without losing sight of a potentially disappointing outcome.

Exercise: How to support internal candidates

- Arrange short meetings with staff asking for your help. Don't be tempted to give them 'just a minute' of your time, as this may derail your existing commitments for the day.
- They may want your take on whether or not to apply for the position. Don't be tempted to say yes or no, as this could really come to haunt you later on.
- Manage expectations by explaining straight away that the meeting is not a guarantee for making the shortlist or securing the position.
- Wait for your member of staff to ask you questions, rather than sharing information and advice right from the start.
- Don't give away too much! If you are engaged in a flowing conversation and you can see real potential, you might be seduced into giving away just a little too much information!
- If you have a number of people interested, why not arrange a group meeting to go through any queries they may have.
- Ignore any veiled or open threats of future resignations if this opportunity does not work out for them. Your candidates are likely to feel the pressure and may say things they come to regret later on.

# # #

Flexible working requests

Doreen* had just nailed her interview. With salary negotiations over, we started discussing her start date.

"I can't work Wednesday mornings, Thursday afternoons or Saturdays and on the whole would prefer night shifts." Doreen's comment caught me off guard, interrupting my explanations about the current rostering system. My colleague Karli* and I exchanged worried glances. We expected staff to work across the year, as the hospital needed staff every hour of every day, all year round. We advised her that we were unable to meet her terms. Doreen* informed us that she would continue her search for a new job, looking for an organisation able to accept her flexible working request.

Exercise: Assessing flexible working requests

Your flexible working policy is your new best friend when navigating the potential minefield that is flexible working. Trying to balance individual preferences with organisational expectations can seem like an impossible task. Your policy should give advice on all of the following:

- Is there a time period staff have to be with you or do they need to pass their probationary period first before they can apply for flexible working?
- What is your process for flexible working requests? Be mindful that even innocent requests can cause havoc when organising the roster. Do you have a system that includes liaising with the roster manager, discussing it with HR and formalising any agreement?
- How do you ensure your decision making is fair when you are desperate for staff? I mention this as there will be talented people, just like Doreen, who will threaten to go to the

competition if you don't agree with their demands. Just like the government has a policy that they won't negotiate with terrorists, it's important for you to have your boundaries. Giving in can be risky business, particularly if you have said no to similar requests from long members of your team.

# # #

How to say no

Your advertisement for the Senior Manager job generated way more applications than you thought it would. After interviewing six outstanding people for the job, you have made your decision. George has the relevant experience, skills and competencies. He has stepped up to the role on numerous occasions and has a likeable personality. All is said and done and there is just one little thing left to do: Contacting the five unsuccessful candidates. It's not a task you are looking forward to. What are you going to say if they ask for a detailed explanation? Even worse, what if they get really angry with you? Should you phone them or invite them for a meeting? Could you get away with just putting out a congratulatory announcement?

Having faced the difficult conversation you have when saying no to someone many times, I have learned that it's never easy. Here are my best strategies for making this situation easier for both parties:

- Let candidates know when and how they will hear from you at the time of the interview. This will ease their anxiety and give you the chance to schedule protected time in your diary.

- Make lots of notes of your observations and thoughts during the interview itself. What captures your interest and imagination? Where is room for improvement? What do you particularly like or dislike? Where did your candidate well and what are areas for improvement?

- How do you measure success, failure and the space in between? A formal scoring system will give you the metrics you need for a detailed analysis you can share with unsuccessful candidates.

- If you are phoning applicants to say no, consider offering a face–to-face meeting to discuss it in person. This is particularly important for internal promotion opportunities. Nobody likes to be rejected and turning a loyal colleague down with a short phone call is not the best way to keep them happy. Staff going for a promotion almost always want to grow and thrive on new challenges. If they are serious about the opportunity, they will have spent hours preparing for the big day. Every day in their current position will have conjured up dreams of doing more, learning more and being more. All of this translates into huge disappointment if they are not the chosen one. Showing your employee that you respect their feelings of frustration will help minimise the risk of talented people leaving.

Exercise: How to prepare to say no

- Go through your interview notes and write down objectively the good, the bad and the ugly. Do stay away from platitudes such as "You did really well, but other people were just better than you!" Focus on giving your candidate constructive feedback they can use to improve and learn for next time.

- The feedback sandwich is often seen as a total management cliché, but it does have the advantage that it follows a clear structure. Start with good news first, add areas for improvement next and finish up on a positive note. You could change this up by sharing important observations you have made, especially if there were points that impressed or surprised you.

- Focus your colleagues' attention on the future by asking what goals they want to achieve in their current position. Is there an opening for them to take on new challenges or responsibilities? Are there options for further training, development or mentorship you can support right now?

- Imagine every single one of your rejected candidates leaves your office feeling excited about the months ahead. How much easier would that make life for you? How likely is it that they forget their feelings of disappointment and focus on adventures yet to come?

# # #

Why you should ask candidates to complete feedback forms

"Oh my goodness, what a total waste of time! The place is in the sticks, there is no bus service and I paid £12 for a taxi. I waited 45 minutes in reception, because one manager was held up in a meeting. When I finally got in the interview room, they told me I'm not suitable for the job. I asked why they invited me in the first place. I learned they were shopping for CV's, to be used if things changed and they needed good people in the future. I couldn't believe it. I was tempted to walk out, but that would have looked really unprofessional. So I answered their questions, you know, for the imaginary job, before starting the long trek home. I don't care if they like me or not, I'm never going to work there. Worst interview ever."

Have you ever sounded like this or know someone who had a story just like that one after your dream job turned into an interview nightmare?

Did you give your feedback to the company you visited or share it with friends and family?

Having the ability to measure objectively the job seekers' experience has as multitude of advantages for you. You get to know how they felt about you and your organisation. You will learn what candidates value the most as well as any concerns they may have.

Exercise: Introducing feedback forms

- Decide what you want to measure and how. Many surveys use the Likert scale as a way of representing people's opinions and attitudes of an experience. You could use simple rating questions, such as "On a scale of 1-5, how would you rate your journey here" combined with information seeking questions such as "How long did you wait in reception?"

- Book a regular time in the diary to analyse the feedback with 2-3 trusted colleagues. Look for any patterns as much as irregularities when analysing the data. Take notes of any negative observations and consider what changes you could implement to turn this around. What could you do to ensure candidates leave on happy terms, regardless of the interview outcome?

- Check how the data you gathered could inform your marketing efforts. If people think highly of your location and transport links, how could you incorporate this into your advertisements? Do you ask applicants if you can put some of their comments on your website?

Chapter 6
Preparing for induction & end of probation

How to organise induction

The ink on the contract has dried. A start date is booked in the calendar. Surely, it must be time to sit back and relax. You probably know from experience that now is not the time to stop for a break. A whole induction programme is waiting to be organised.

Many participants in my workshop tell me that recruitment is not a problem for them-it's staff retention that's causing a constant headache. The business directory defines staff retention as:"an effort by a business to maintain a working environment which supports current staff in remaining with the company". That task starts the day new employees take their seat ready to be trained for the job. A search for 'how to organise induction training' delivered plenty of downloadable tools, templates and blogs. This proves organisations across the globe recognise the importance of creating positive working relationships from day one.

Exercise: How to organise successful induction training

Many new starters will be filled with doubt and excitement in equal measure. Will this job be right for them? Will they be happy here? Have they made the right decision when they handed in that resignation letter at their last place of work? What if they fail to make the grade? Only time will tell the answers to any of these questions. You can help them disburse some of these doubts, have confidence in their choices and settle more quickly into their role by delivering a well thought-out induction programme.

Basic components of induction training:

Practical aspects: shift routines, break times, how to request holidays, sickness/absence policies, contact details, fire exits and arrangements for refreshments.

Organisational aspects: your mission and vision, goals, values, philosophy, routines, ethics, diversity, safety rules and policies.

Statutory - and mandatory - training: What do people need to learn to do the job? The combination of courses will depend on your specific workplace. Your government or regulator will require for all staff to complete range of health and safety at work courses. You may also have a set of mandatory courses employees need to do the job safely and effectively.

On the job training: mentor-and preceptorship including workbooks, shadowing people, buddy system

Evaluation: feedback forms with rating scales, review meetings in staggered intervals (two weeks, three months, six months followed by regular supervisions and yearly appraisal)

End of probation meetings

The agitation was visible in Harry's* face as he quickly sat down. His heart was racing as his eyes darted across the room to the two people holding the power to make or break his future. Trying to control his breathing, he took a slow breath and waited for them to cast their verdict...

Do you remember the last time you attended an end of probation meeting? Did you have a similar experience to Harry* or did you already know you would pass? Have you ever been informed your probation needed to be extended without any warning signs beforehand?

The end of probation meeting is always a highly emotive meeting, no matter what side of the table you are sitting on. You may encounter total devastation when you have to extend or fail the probationary period. You can tell how much it means when new employees grow with confidence right before your eyes when told they have made the grade.

Exercise: How to prepare for End of Probation meetings

End of Probation meetings require diligent preparation, as there is a lot at stake from both a personal, as well as legal perspective. Carrying out a detailed analysis of all the intelligence you have received so far is essential to reaching an objective decision. You may want to gather feedback from mentors, clients and colleagues, review sickness/absence levels, check the mentorship/preceptorship book and evaluate any complaints and compliments.

Mentorship/Preceptorship Workbooks:

I have sat in plenty of these meetings to know that new employees tend to forget, misplace or present an incomplete workbook. This can be quite frustrating, especially when you are sitting on the fence and you haven't quite made your mind up what to do next. Check your HR and induction policies to make sure the consequences of not completing the workbook are clearly laid out for new starters. Taking a firm stance on this issue will protect you from unnecessary disputes later down the line.

Passing probation:

There doesn't seem much to do apart from congratulating your employee, signing the piece of paper and extending a warm welcome to the newest addition to your team. It's good to remember at this point that one of our human drives is the need to learn and be challenged. The induction period is a constant adventure filled with new impressions, goals and obstacles. You can extend these high levels of accomplishment, motivation and performance by agreeing exciting and achievable goals with employees before they leave the meeting.

Extending probation:

Telling someone that their probationary time has been extended or failed, and therefore putting their financial security at risk takes a lot of confidence, courage and commitment. It is essential that you absolute trust in your final decision before getting together with your employee. You will also want to prepare yourself mentally, as some staff will attempt to blame you for their shortcomings.

Staff members may turn up in your office, completely oblivious that something is wrong. Others have a good insight, but don't want to accept the predicament they are facing. Individuals may attempt to persuade you to let them pass, promising to try harder from now on. It's worth mentioning that some people can turn quite volatile when things don't go to plan, and you need to make arrangements to stay safe at all times. Just like with appraisal meetings, you don't want to deliver bad news completely out of the blue.

Ask yourself if and how your team member knows that they are not achieving their performance targets. Have you had a documented discussion with them previously? Is this person aware what they would need to do and in which time-frame for the successful completion of their trial period?

Always ensure another colleague, preferably from the personnel department, is with you and takes notes during the conversation. This will eliminate the risk of employees becoming hostile or aggressive towards you. Written minutes with documented goals are essential to support staff in reaching their personal -and professional - targets. You may also need to refer to them if you need to fail probation leading to legal challenges later on.

Be familiar with your capability policies and the Equality Act 2010: All organisations are prohibited from discriminatory practices. The Equality Act 2010 collates together different pieces of legislation to promote equal treatment for everybody. It is your responsibility as an employer to put in place reasonable adjustments. Staff do not have a legal obligation to declare individual circumstances or health conditions covered by the Act. You may run into difficulties if you want to extend or fail someone's probationary period and they disclose in the meeting that they need additional support. It is imperative that you do not make any decisions before consulting your HR -and Occupational Health department for assistance. You may have to re-schedule the appointment until you have received further advice and guidance.

Failing probationary period:

Never, ever, fail someone's probation by yourself. I know I have told you this before. I am telling you again as I have seen my fair share of placid staff erupting into angry volcanoes when they heard the news. There will be times when an employment contract has to end right there and then. Every organisation has their own policies outlining what counts as gross misconduct, warranting instant dismissal. Common examples include: criminal acts, aggressive or violent behaviour, theft of company property, threatening behaviour or turning up to work intoxicated. Consult with your Personnel department and line manager to develop a plan of action. If there is evidence of criminal activity, you may need to contact the police right away.

A more common scenario is the member of staff failing to meet their agreed objectives. People in this situation will often plead with you for another chance, so that they can provide food on the table for their family. This can be absolutely heart-breaking and staying firm is really easier said than done. If you find yourself in that position, it's essential that you keep calm and professional by steering the conversation back on topic. You can do this by summarising how previous measures did not achieve the desired outcome.

Practice beforehand what to say to wrap up the conversation to prevent the discussion going round in circles or off track.

Pick your time carefully as the ties of working contracts tend to be severed immediately. Don't make the mistake of arranging appointments in the morning, expecting employees to still work the rest of their shift. You might need to organise additional cover to balance out potential staffing shortfalls.

Chapter 7

The best staff retention strategies

Staff retention strategies

Choosing the right person for the job is just the first step in your quest of creating a thriving workforce. What counts just as much are all the strategies you put in place to persuade people to stay. Staff retention is a huge topic, and I won't even attempt to cover it here. I do want, however, to share with you my best staff retention ideas in the hope that they will help you achieve your own personal -and professional goals.

# # #

Do you know why people stay?
Do you know why staff stay with you, even though local competitors are doing everything they can to tempt them away from you?

I always ask this question in my workshops, and it never fails me to amaze me that no one seems to know for sure. It appears that it's very rare for companies to collect staff retention data. Having a clear understanding of the reasons people remain with you has a multitude of advantages. You can use it to build trust and improve the effectiveness of your marketing messages. You are able to determine the deciding factors in influencing loyalty and promoting a positive company culture.

Everyone seems to have a clear process in place for finding out why people wanted to leave. Reducing staff turnover and improving retention is a goal shared by many organisations and finding the answers seems to be shrouded in mystery.

Annual staff satisfaction surveys measure current motivation levels and feedback how to improve things. They still don't tell you what you can do to persuade people to stay.

I am confident that staff retention data will take on a new level of importance as competition for talented staff increases. I also believe that existing staff will become more involved in marketing vacancies as people stop believing the corporate message. Every service will want to exploit their unique selling points for clients and staff alike.

Think about how you, your department and your organisation would benefit from an in-depth look at staff retention. How could you use this research to inform your recruitment decisions?

What financial business goals and objectives could you achieve if you could incorporate this intelligence into your marketing materials?

How could you use the insights you have to influence your current strategy and relationships with internal or external stakeholders?

Exercise:

Step 1: Write down the names of six colleagues, who have been with your organisation three years or more. Ask yourself 'Why is this person still working here?" Consider if they got promotions, additional training, live locally or have special interests or expertise. Write down as much as you can. What do they like about working for your organisation?

Step 2: Ask them!

Step 3: Compare notes. How did your guesswork match with the feedback you got from each person? Where did it match up and how did it differ from your assumptions? Did you gain any vital clues you could use to support your current goals and objectives?

You might be wondering why this exercise is only limited to three people, considering your staff count is in the hundreds. Douglas W. Hubbard suggests in his book "How to measure anything" that you only need to analyse data from 6 people to obtain an average measurement of the group as a whole.

# # #

Supervision: How to rescue meetings when you get stuck

How often do you hear people say they are "fine" and they are really "fine?" Exactly!
I remember the day I had my first supervision meeting. I was so excited. I had done the training, I was well prepared, I was ready- until my member of staff arrived. The form had quite a lot of questions covered everything from patient experience to working with colleagues. Unfortunately, my member of staff answered all questions with just one word "Fine". Here are some examples and coaching tools you can use to overcome barriers of communication.

1.) "I've had enough. I don't always want to be the one picking up all the work."

What do you want instead? From what you are saying, it looks like you want to ensure work is shared out fairly?

"Nothing is going right. No matter what I do, there is just endless criticism"

Imagine you are in the cinema, watching a day at work like a movie. Can you pick up the moments where things are going the way you want them to be?
What are they? Who is there with you? Make those pictures 3D and observe. What's different?

"Everything is fine"
If you could change one thing around here, what would it be?

- Imagine I have asked you to write a note with three things you want to discuss today last night. What would the note say?

"I'm not going anywhere in this organisation. My skills are just wasted"

- Get a piece of paper and a pen and draw a timeline starting from the date your member of staff joined the organisation. Mark the dates of completing induction, End of Probation, first ward round, first CPA meeting, first supervision meeting, first appraisal, any projects....ask the member of staff what other moments stand out for them and why. What skills have they used? What experience gained? Have they got other moments that really stood out for them? What was special?
- Move the line into the future. Ask your member of staff to put markers in with dates and what skills, knowledge and experience they would like to gain between now and then

"Nobody cares about the work we do. We've put everything into this project and now it's scrapped thanks to budget cuts."

Ask your colleague about someone they really admire and just for a moment pretend this person is coming to visit to find out everything they can about this project. How did it start? What went really well? Highlights?

- What challenges did you face? How did you overcome them? If it was a story, what would need to happen to give it a happy ending?

# # #

Heike's story

I left it till the end of the book to tell you a little more about me and my journey. I arrived in the UK in 1999, having just qualified as a nurse for people with Intellectual Disabilities. Job opportunities were far and few between back home, and it was always my dream to work here. I worked as a Support Worker until my qualifications were recognised by the Nursing -and Midwifery Council. Once that happened, there was no stopping me. I quickly moved up the career ladder, working with different client groups and running my own department in 2014. Recruiting and retaining staff became the key focus of my working life. It's impossible to provide high standards in the service industry without dedicated employees. I went through the highs of filling all of my vacancies to full establishment. I also experienced the lows, when new service developments saw me recruiting 50 staff in just 90 days. I reviewed hundreds of applications, interviewed more candidates than I can remember and tinkered endlessly with the system to attract, recruit and retain the best people for the job. A serious health scare and subsequent redundancy led me into a versatile career as an author, speaker, healthcare professional and trainer specialised in recruitment and retention. I want to share with you what I've learned so far. I believe that taking even one or two snippets of advice and applying them to your own setting can transform your situation and achieve measurable change.

I would love to hear how you are getting on. You can contact me with questions, comments and feedback here: heike@thecoachingnurse.com

I answer all of my e-mails personally and look forward to hearing from you.

All the best,

Heike

PS: Don't forget to download your free recruitment checklist right here: www.goagencyfree.com/recruitment-day

# # #

Further resources:

Top #10 Amazon Bestseller: **How To Fill 50 Jobs In 90 Days**

Whether you are new to recruitment, an experienced recruiter or struggling to recruit in a crowded market, 'How To Fill 50 Jobs In 90 Days' is a step-by-step guide on how you can achieve your recruitment goals as well as personal –and professional success. Written specifically for professionals wanting to recruit the best people for the job when budgets are right, you'll learn how to secure financial gains and win great staff in competitive markets. Follow the recruitment process from advert to interview, learn how to roll out responsive e-mail campaigns, use Social Media techniques to build your contact list, reduce the risk of employing the wrong person and negotiate contracts with confidence. Available here:
https://www.amazon.co.uk/dp/B01MQONV3K/

Recruitment on a budget workshops

Recruitment on a budget workshops work in partnership with professionals working in the health-and social care sector to fill vacancies and go agency free. This training gives you a proven, evidence -based system to plan out cost -effective recruitment campaigns in a competitive climate.

Learning outcomes:

- How to assess your recruitment needs and locate suitable candidates
- How to carry out a detailed analysis of your competitors in the market
- How to tailor your marketing message and engage applicants online and offline
- How to accelerate your Social Media efforts and build a candidate pipeline
- How to create value -based interviews and structure recruitment days
- How to negotiate a win -win deal and secure the best people for the job

Find out more about the workshops and get in touch here: www.goagencyfree.com/events

Quote 'Recruitment' on the contact form for a 10% discount!

Fill your vacancies online

Do you feel nervous about your next finance meeting? Are you swamped with application forms, but only a handful of them are suitable? Is your recruitment budget wiped out by agency fees and you don't have time to attend a workshop? If you have answered yes to any of these questions, it's time to claim back your sanity and your desk! Learn everything you need to build a high -profile recruitment campaign online. With plenty of videos, downloadable templates and a great workbook, this course has everything you need to plan your next campaign from start to finish. Get started for free and access all the resources from Module 1 right here: www.goagencyfree.com

Free resources:

Check out www.goagencyfree.com for free resources to attract, recruit and retain the best people for the job!

Made in the USA
Middletown, DE
15 September 2018